CW01073114

Original title:
Healing Wounds

Author: Kaido Väinamäe
ISBN HARDBACK: 978-9916-79-072-4
ISBN PAPERBACK: 978-9916-79-073-1
ISBN EBOOK: 978-9916-79-074-8

Light After Darkness

In shadow's clutch, we often fight,
Yet hope will rise with morning light.
The dawn dispels our deepest fears,
A whisper soft, it calms our tears.

In every heart where pain resides,
There burns a flame that gently guides.
Through trials faced, the spirit grows,
As warmth surrounds, the courage flows.

Each step we take, a path anew,
The strength within will see us through.
As dark retreats and peace draws near,
We find our truth, we conquer fear.

Embrace the day, let worries fade,
For in this light, our fears will trade.
With open hearts, we greet the sun,
In unity, our souls are one.

The Gentle Touch of Kindness

A smile can bridge so wide a gap,
A hand outstretched, a forceful tap.
With words that heal and hearts aligned,
We share a bond, a spark entwined.

In moments brief, we leave a mark,
Each gesture brightens up the dark.
Through simple acts, the world can change,
In love's embrace, no heart feels strange.

As kindness flows, compassion grows,
It sprouts anew like blooming rose.
With gentle hearts, we make a stand,
Together strong, we join our hands.

For every soul beneath the weight,
A tender touch can liberate.
In kindness shared, we rise as one,
In unity, our battles won.

Songs for the Broken

In silence deep, the heart can sing,
A melody from pain takes wing.
Each note, a cry for hope and grace,
A journey shared, we find our place.

The shards of dreams may seem absurd,
But woven close, they form a word.
In harmony, the broken heal,
Together strong, we learn to feel.

With every story, every tear,
The echoes show that love is near.
The music flows, our spirits soar,
In shared embrace, we are much more.

So let us sing, though wounded still,
The songs of hope, the strength of will.
For joy resides in every heart,
In unity, we rise, not part.

Waters of Restoration

A river flows through hearts once dry,
With gentle waves, it lifts the sigh.
In liquid grace, the burdens fade,
A soothing balm, it gently laid.

Where sorrows linger, waters dance,
In depth of wounds, they find their chance.
Restoring hope, reviving dreams,
In tranquil paths, the spirit beams.

Through every storm, a lesson learned,
In currents deep, the tide has turned.
The past may linger, dark and cold,
But in the flow, life's truth unfolds.

So let us drink from streams of grace,
In every drop, our fears we face.
For waters pure bring life anew,
In every heart, a love so true.

Constellations of Courage

In the dark, stars gleam bright,
Guiding hearts in their flight.
Every sparkle tells a tale,
Of those who rise, who prevail.

Fears dissolve in the night air,
With each moment, we declare,
Strength within, a blazing fire,
Heartbeats loud, they never tire.

We walk paths less traveled wide,
With faith as our steadfast guide.
Each step forward, bold and free,
Unlocking our destiny.

Through storms fierce and shadows long,
We find the rhythm, the song.
Together we stand, hand in hand,
A united, fearless band.

So look up, let courage soar,
In constellations, find your core.
For in the sky, our dreams shine bright,
Illuminating the path of light.

Tides of Transformation

Waves roll in, whisper their song,
Carrying dreams where they belong.
The shores shift with every swell,
A reminder that change is well.

The moon's pull dances on the sea,
Inviting growth, bold and free.
Each wave crashes, cleanses the sand,
Transforming the landscape so grand.

In still waters, reflections clear,
Hidden depths, not to fear.
Embrace the flow, let currents guide,
In every ebb, there's hope inside.

Seas of doubt may rise and swell,
But ride the tide, cast your spell.
With every crest, rise up tall,
Embracing change, we shall not fall.

For life's journey is ever-paced,
In the tides, our dreams interlaced.
So sail forth and chase the dawn,
In transformation, we are reborn.

Quiet Resurgence

Amidst the noise, stillness sings,
In whispers, the heart takes wings.
Finding peace in gentle sighs,
Within the calm, the spirit flies.

Beneath the surface, roots remain,
In quiet depths, we break the chain.
A resurgence from the ground,
In silent strength, hope is found.

Softly blooms the springtime flower,
In hidden hours, it draws power.
With each petal, a story unfolds,
Of resilience, quiet and bold.

In the shadows, dreams ignite,
Illuminating the peaceful night.
Through gentle steps and heartfelt grace,
We embrace each sacred space.

So take a breath, let stillness be,
In the quiet, you're truly free.
Let the world around you pause,
In resurgence, find your cause.

Mosaic of Memories

Fragments of time, colors blend,
In a mosaic that has no end.
Each shard tells of joy and pain,
A tapestry of love's refrain.

Scattered moments, bright and dim,
Piecing together, the light within.
Through laughter shared and tears we shed,
A gallery of things unsaid.

Layers deep, the heart does see,
Every memory sets us free.
In the chaos, find the art,
Each piece a map, a treasured part.

Through time's lens, we grow and change,
Yet the essence will never estrange.
The past cradles who we are,
In the quilted glow of a distant star.

So cherish each moment, woven tight,
In the fabric of day and night.
A mosaic of life we create,
From memories cherished, never late.

The Language of Resilience

In the quiet, strength is found,
Every heartbeat a silent sound.
We rise again from ashes grey,
With hope as our guiding ray.

Roots dig deep in hardened ground,
Through storms and trials, we are bound.
Voices whisper, tales untold,
In every bruise, a heart of gold.

Mountains loom, yet we stand tall,
In unity, we break the fall.
Through tears we weave a tapestry,
A story stitched in bravery.

With every setback, we embrace,
This dance of life, a bold grace.
In shadows cast, we still ignite,
A flame that shines through darkest night.

So let the winds of change blow strong,
In the rhythm, we find our song.
With courage as our steadfast shield,
The language of resilience revealed.

Dances of Release

In twilight's glow, we shed our fears,
With every twirl, we shed the years.
The music calls, our spirits rise,
In every step, the soul complies.

Gentle breezes can set us free,
As we sway to the symphony.
With open hearts, we find our flow,
In this dance, emotions glow.

Twisting, turning, letting go,
In the moment, feelings show.
Through laughter's echo, joy is found,
In our hearts, the world unbound.

The shadows fade, and light breaks through,
In every leap, something anew.
We find release in each embrace,
Freedom lives in this sacred space.

So take my hand, let's lose our cares,
As we move to rhythms rare.
In this dance of life, we're whole,
United in body and soul.

Glimmers in the Chaos

Amidst the storm, a spark will gleam,
A flicker in the wildest dream.
Through swirling winds, we learn to see,
The beauty in the mayhem's spree.

Fragments swirl like autumn leaves,
Yet in the mess, the heart believes.
Glimmers shine through darkest nights,
In chaos wrapped, a dance of lights.

With every pulse, a heartbeat sings,
In tangled webs, we find our wings.
Moments brief yet fiercely bright,
Guiding us through the endless night.

So breathe it in, the swirling awe,
In every struggle, there's a flaw.
Glimmers beckon, calling clear,
Embrace the chaos, hold it dear.

For in the chaos, life unfolds,
With every tale, a picture holds.
In the light, we learn to be,
Glimmers found in unity.

The Pathway to Wholeness

Within the heart, a journey starts,
With every step, we mend the parts.
Through winding roads, we seek the truth,
In the embrace of our lost youth.

Stars guide us on this path so wide,
In silence, we learn to abide.
With open arms, we greet our flaws,
In the stillness, we find the cause.

Each lesson learned, a treasure gained,
In every heartache, love unchained.
Together we walk this sacred trail,
As shadows fade, we shall not pale.

Through sunlit paths and moonlit dreams,
We navigate the silent streams.
The essence of life, a gentle call,
We rise, we stumble, we won't fall.

The pathway twists yet leads us home,
In every heart, we shall not roam.
For wholeness lies within our reach,
In every moment, life will teach.

The Art of Mending

In pieces we are often found,
With edges sharp and raw, unbound.
Yet gentle hands can sew the fray,
Transforming night into bright day.

The fabric tells of tales untold,
Of warmth and strength in threads of gold.
With patience, needle finds its way,
To stitch the heart, come what may.

Each tear a mark of battles strong,
A testament we still belong.
In mending, love begins to weave,
A tapestry that we believe.

The art requires both heart and skill,
To mend the break, to shape the will.
With every knot, a bond is made,
In threads of hope, we will not fade.

So gather up the frayed and worn,
From sorrow, joy will yet be born.
In mending hearts, we find the start,
Of every piece, a work of art.

Woven Threads of Resilience

In fabric worn from storms endured,
Threads of resilience have emerged.
Each color bright, a story shared,
In patterns, strength our hearts declared.

From darkest nights the dawn will rise,
Woven tales beneath the skies.
In every stitch, we find the hope,
That lifts our spirits, helps us cope.

Through trials faced and battles fought,
The threads of life have lessons taught.
In woven arcs, we hold our dreams,
Resilience flows in vibrant streams.

Together strong, no thread alone,
In unity, our courage grown.
Through woven paths, we find the way,
To greet the dawn of a new day.

Each challenge faced, a thread we add,
In this design, we won't feel sad.
For in our strength, the beauty shows,
In woven threads, our spirit glows.

Light Through the Cracks

In shadows deep where whispers lie,
A flicker fights, a silent cry.
Through cracks and seams, the light will break,
Awakening hope for our own sake.

The darkness holds a fleeting sway,
Yet beams of grace can find the way.
In every fracture, warmth will shine,
Illumining paths, our lives entwine.

Each crack a testament to strife,
Yet through the gaps, we find new life.
Potential born from what we hide,
A tender place for dreams to bide.

So let the light come seeping through,
In every shade, embrace the hue.
For in the fractures, stories speak,
Of strength and courage in the weak.

In daylight's grace, we find our peace,
From brokenness, our hearts release.
Through cracks, we'll see the beauty form,
A testament to weathering the storm.

Songs of the Soul's Restoration

In quiet moments, echoes rise,
Songs of the heart, a sweet surprise.
Melodies that heal the soul,
Restoring grace, making us whole.

Each note a balm for scars we bear,
Resounding through the stillness, rare.
Harmony blooms in fragile space,
A symphony of love and grace.

Through trials deep and sorrows cast,
The music flows, it holds us fast.
In rhythms soft, we find relief,
A song that carries through our grief.

With every harmony, we rise,
In chorus bright, beneath the skies.
The soul's restoration, a gentle art,
In every note, the path to heart.

So sing our songs, let voices blend,
With every echo, spirits mend.
In melodies, we find our way,
Restoration leads, come what may.

A Song of the Undone

In shadows deep, where dreams reside,
The tales of loss and hopes abide.
Silent whispers weave through air,
A melody of despair's despair.

Once bright horizons fade to grey,
As time slips softly, day by day.
Yet in the heart, a spark persists,
A song of life, that still exists.

Through aching voids and haunted nights,
Resilience blooms, ignites its lights.
Though paths may twist, and time may bend,
A song is sung, it knows no end.

With every falter, every fall,
We rise anew, we heed the call.
For in the undone, beauty swells,
In brokenness, the heart still dwells.

So sing we now, through pain and strife,
A chorus bold, the pulse of life.
Together still, we'll find our way,
In the undone, we choose to stay.

Embrace of the Past

In gentle folds of time's embrace,
The echoes linger, soft in grace.
Memories dance like autumn leaves,
Woven deep, the heart believes.

Whispers of laughter, tears of old,
Stories told, both meek and bold.
In shadows long, the light still glows,
The past, a river, freely flows.

Embrace the scars, for they are lines,
Maps of journeys, the heart designs.
In every tear, wisdom shines bright,
A tapestry of dark and light.

Nostalgia wraps like a warm shawl,
Comfort found in the rise and fall.
Though moments slip like grains of sand,
The past remains, a guiding hand.

So let us cherish the paths we've trod,
In every memory, we find a nod.
For in the past, our spirits soar,
An embrace eternal, forevermore.

Light Through the Cracks

In battered walls where shadows creep,
A fractured world begins to weep.
Yet through the fissures, hope finds way,
Dancing light at break of day.

The cracks are stories, damage told,
In silent whispers, brave and bold.
A testament to strength unseen,
In brokenness, the heart can glean.

Illuminated by the scars,
A glimpse of grace beneath the stars.
Through thickest veils, the light breaks free,
Guiding souls toward what can be.

Each jagged edge, a pathway bright,
Leading forth from darkest night.
In every flaw, a beauty seen,
The cracks hold secrets, lush and green.

So let the light through shadows pour,
Resilience found in every core.
In cracks we find, life's vibrant track,
A dance of hope, our guiding knack.

The Silence of Mending

In quiet spaces, mending starts,
A gentle balm for broken parts.
In stillness deep, the soul takes breath,
Embracing life amidst the death.

Threads of gold weave through the pain,
Crafting hope from the darkest strain.
Each whispered word a sacred pact,
Awakening all that we unpack.

In solitude's embrace, we grow,
Healing petals, soft as snow.
The silence sings a soothing tune,
A lullaby beneath the moon.

With each repair, we find our grace,
The art of time, a tender space.
In mending hearts, we learn to see,
That love remains, forever free.

So speak in silence, let it mend,
For in the quiet, we transcend.
In every crack, a story flows,
The silence holds, as healing grows.

A Tapestry of Scars

In whispered shadows, stories unfold,
Threads of pain, in silence retold.
Each mark a journey, each line a fight,
Woven together, they shimmer in light.

A tapestry rich, in colors so bold,
Moments of sorrow, and strength to behold.
Through the darkness, resilience gleams,
A testament echoing, the power of dreams.

Beneath the surface, the heartbeats cry,
In the fabric of life, scars never lie.
We wear them like armor, a shield against fears,
Crafted with patience, mixed with our tears.

Each scar a chapter, a piece of the whole,
Mapping our journeys, stitching the soul.
From ashes of sorrow, new hope is spun,
A beautiful quilt, where we all become one.

Fragments of Hope

In the quiet corners, hope starts to dwell,
Whispers of light, casting shadows from hell.
A broken heart mends with threads of gold,
Crafted in dreams, and stories retold.

Each fragment a beacon, a guiding star bright,
Piercing the darkness, igniting the night.
In every heartbeat, a promise we'll keep,
We rise from the ashes, and no longer weep.

Hope dances gently, on wings made of grace,
Creating a refuge, a warm, safe space.
With hands intertwined, we nurture the spark,
Together we shine, even in the dark.

And when the world trembles, and shadows grow long,
We sing of our strength, we sing our own song.
For in every whisper, and every small sigh,
Fragments of hope, will never say die.

Sowing Seeds of Solace

In fields of the heart, we plant with care,
Seeds of compassion, watered with prayer.
Through trials and troubles, we nurture the ground,
Finding solace in whispers, where peace can be found.

Each moment a blessing, a chance to grow,
From shadows of sorrow, new blooms start to show.
Tender shoots rising, reaching for skies,
In the garden of healing, love never dies.

A patchwork of kindness, where laughter will reign,
Harvesting beauty from echoes of pain.
With every season, new stories will weave,
A tapestry thriving, for those who believe.

Sowing seeds of solace, each heart is a bloom,
Together we brighten, dispelling the gloom.
In the warmth of the sun, and the love we share,
A garden of hope, grows lush and rare.

Cracks in the Armor

Beneath the bravado, the shields that we bear,
Lies a world of wonder, of courage laid bare.
In cracks of the armor, the light starts to seep,
Revealing the stories, we longed not to keep.

Each fissure a glimpse, of battles once fought,
A reminder that vulnerability is not for naught.
Through moments of doubt, we learn to embrace,
The strength in our struggles, the beauty of grace.

With open hearts, we weave from the pain,
Transforming our scars into wisdom gained.
In the fractures, we find a new way to thrive,
For it's in our softness, that we feel alive.

So let us wear proudly, the cracks that we show,
An emblem of courage, in the ebb and the flow.
For through every break, we find ways to mend,
Turning wounds into stories, making hearts ascend.

Gentle Thorns

In the garden where shadows lie,
Petals bloom but thorns still pry.
Soft whispers from the leaves above,
Speak of pain yet cradle love.

Morning dew like tears do gleam,
On fragile hopes, we dare to dream.
Roots entwined beneath the ground,
Silent battles often found.

Hues of red against the green,
Beauty veils what lies unseen.
Every heart that dares to feel,
Learns that love and hurt can heal.

In the twilight's gentle kiss,
Moments passed that we won't miss.
For every thorn that pricks the skin,
A stronger spirit waits within.

So in the garden, take your stance,
Embrace the thorns, and join the dance.
For every hurt that shapes our form,
Is but a sign of love reborn.

The Phoenix's Dance

From ashes cold, a flame ignites,
A tale of loss that boldly fights.
Wings of fire, they stretch and soar,
In death's embrace, we find much more.

With every breath, the embers rise,
A resurrection in the skies.
Singing songs of ancient lore,
Where hope has burned forevermore.

Each feather glows with vibrant light,
In shadows deep, they dare to fight.
Through trials fierce and tempests fierce,
A spirit strong, we'll not be pierced.

In the dance of flames, we spin,
Releasing all that lies within.
From every crack, new life will bloom,
In stillness found, we break the gloom.

So rise, dear heart, in endless flight,
Embrace the day, embrace the night.
For in this cycle, life will trance,
With every fall, the Phoenix's dance.

Stitches of the Soul

In hidden seams where secrets lay,
A tapestry of night and day.
Threads of sorrow, threads of grace,
Woven tight in a sacred space.

Needles pierce with tender care,
Mending hearts laid bare, aware.
Every knot, a whispered tale,
Of battles fought, and dreams set sail.

Through every tear, a glimpse of light,
Stitched together, wrongs made right.
In the fabric of our days,
Hope emerges in myriad ways.

So gather close, these stitches fine,
A pattern forged, forever mine.
For in the fray, we find our whole,
Embracing the stitches of the soul.

Through colors bright and shadows deep,
In this quilt of love, we keep.
Each patch a story, rich and bold,
Crafted gently, stitched with gold.

Embracing the Fractured

In fragments lost, we find our grace,
Each shattered piece a sacred space.
A puzzle formed from broken dreams,
In chaos whispers softest themes.

With open arms, we hold the scars,
Embracing light from distant stars.
For every crack, a story grows,
Therein lies beauty no one knows.

Through gentle hands, we touch the pain,
In every loss, a chance to gain.
For brokenness can shape the whole,
A testament to a resilient soul.

In unity where fragments meet,
A heartfelt rhythm, bittersweet.
Finding strength in what was torn,
A new creation is reborn.

So let us dance in fractured light,
With every step, we face the night.
Together we rise, forever bold,
Embracing all that life unfolds.

Carving New Paths

Amidst the thorns, we pave our way,
With courage firm, we do not sway.
The dawn breaks bright, a brand new start,
In every step, we play our part.

Rivers rush with stories untold,
Through valleys deep, we brave the cold.
Each stone we lift, each shade we greet,
We carve the paths beneath our feet.

The mountains call with whispered dreams,
Above the clouds, the sunlight beams.
Together strong, we climb and rise,
With hope as vast as open skies.

The road ahead is yet untraced,
In every heart, our dreams embraced.
With passion's fire, we go ahead,
To carve new paths where few have tread.

So take my hand, let's share the view,
In this journey, we will renew.
As seasons change and moments last,
We're forging futures, unsurpassed.

Reclaimed by the Light

In shadows deep, the heart will roam,
Yet every path can lead us home.
With gentle hands, we heal the scars,
As day breaks bright beneath the stars.

The night can chill, but warmth will rise,
With every dawn, we claim the skies.
When darkness fades, new hope is spun,
Reborn in light, we start to run.

The whispers of the past will fade,
As sunlight glows, foundations laid.
Awake the dreams that softly gleam,
In every breath, we forge our dream.

No fear should haunt, nor doubt contrive,
In light's embrace, we truly thrive.
With every smile, a spark ignites,
Reclaimed by love, we chase the lights.

So dance with joy, let spirits soar,
In every heart, we seek for more.
With open arms, we face the day,
For in the light, we find our way.

Soothe of the Earth

Beneath the trees, a whisper calls,
In gentle tones, the silence falls.
The breeze carries a soft caress,
In nature's arms, we find our rest.

With every rustle, peace we seek,
In soothing shades, the world feels meek.
The rivers sing their tranquil song,
In harmony, we all belong.

Among the flowers, colors bright,
Their fragrance dances in the light.
With every step on soil so rich,
We find our balance, heal the pitch.

The sun dips low, the shadows grow,
In twilight's glow, our worries go.
With every heartbeat, bond so pure,
The Earth's embrace, our spirits cure.

So when the day slows down its pace,
In nature's lap, we find our grace.
With open hearts, we walk the mirth,
In the soothing touch of the Earth.

The Heart's Patchwork

In pieces stitched from days gone by,
Each square a tale, a heartfelt sigh.
Threads of laughter, woven tight,
In the patchwork glow, we find our light.

From every sorrow, every ache,
A tapestry of vows we make.
With colors bold and soft shades too,
The heart's patchwork tells what's true.

Moments cherished, memories spun,
In the fabric of the love we've won.
Together brave, through stormy weather,
Our quilt of hope, we craft together.

Every stitch a prayer, a wish,
In the patterns, we find our bliss.
As years unfold, the seams won't tire,
The heart's patchwork, a boldly lit fire.

So gather close, in warmth we find,
The beauty in the ties that bind.
For in this quilt, our souls entwine,
The heart's patchwork, forever shine.

Winds of Change

Beneath the sky so wide and blue,
The winds begin to stir anew.
They whisper secrets, tales to share,
Of journeys bold, beyond compare.

They lift the leaves, they dance the trees,
A gentle breath, a playful breeze.
With every gust, old dreams take flight,
And guide us into the soft twilight.

As seasons shift, they forge ahead,
A promise speaks where once we tread.
Through valleys deep and mountains tall,
The winds of change will call us all.

Each step we take, a mark we leave,
In whispered tones, we come to believe.
That though the world may twist and bend,
Our hearts will guide us to the end.

So feel the winds, embrace the roam,
For in their dance, we find our home.
With courage, hope, and open eyes,
The winds of change will never die.

Nestled in Comfort

Inside these walls, a warmth resides,
A gentle glow that love provides.
With every corner, stories spun,
Nestled in comfort, we are one.

The laughter echoes, sweet and clear,
Each moment cherished, held so dear.
The hearth's embrace, the softest bed,
In this cocoon, our worries shed.

Through storms that rage and nights so long,
In comfort's arms, we grow more strong.
A haven built with hearts and hands,
Here in this space, true joy expands.

So let the world outside remain,
As bliss surrounds, dispelling pain.
Together, wrapped in love's warm thread,
Nestled in comfort, softly fed.

With every sunrise, hope ignites,
In cozy whispers, dreams take flight.
Together here, we boldly stand,
In this sweet comfort, hand in hand.

Threads of Tomorrow

With every choice, a thread we weave,
In patterns bright, our minds believe.
Each moment spins a story fine,
In threads of tomorrow, we intertwine.

Visions dance in colors bold,
Futures waiting to unfold.
With courage sewn in every seam,
We stitch together every dream.

A tapestry of hopes and fears,
Woven gently through the years.
Each thread a path, both rough and clear,
Leading us to what we hold dear.

Through trials faced, through joy and pain,
Our threads connect, a sweet refrain.
And though the end is yet unseen,
We trust the fabric we have gleaned.

So let us weave with heart and soul,
In threads of tomorrow, we are whole.
For in this work, we learn to grow,
In every stitch, our spirits glow.

The Unseen Tides

Beyond the shores, a mystery waits,
The unseen tides that shift the fates.
With gentle pull, the ocean sighs,
In whispered waves, our longing lies.

They ebb and flow, a hidden dance,
In every ripple, fate's romance.
The moonlight guides their secret play,
Drawing hearts, come what may.

Beneath the surface, currents roam,
In unseen depths, we find our home.
Though tides may rise, or fall away,
Their call persists in night and day.

So let us heed the ocean's song,
For in the tides, we all belong.
With open hearts and minds anew,
Embrace the change, let it ensue.

For every wave that kisses land,
A promise waits, a guiding hand.
Through unseen tides, our spirits glide,
In faith and trust, we shall abide.

Inside the Softening

In twilight's glow, the colors blend,
Whispers of warmth gently descend.
A silence wraps the world in grace,
As shadows dance, a soft embrace.

The heart unlocks a tender door,
Each sigh a promise, so much more.
The petals fall, the earth inhales,
In every moment, love prevails.

The stars awaken in the night,
Painting dreams in silver light.
Weaving threads of hope anew,
In softening skies, we find our view.

Where echoes of the past remain,
In gentle moments, we feel no pain.
The hands of time caress our face,
Within this warmth, we find our place.

So gather close, to share our tales,
In the softening, love prevails.
Through every heartache, every tear,
Together, we will conquer fear.

Shadows Reclaimed

In the depth of night, shadows breathe,
Silent whispers, secrets sheathe.
A dance begins where dreams reside,
As lost hopes flow with the tide.

Echoes linger, stories unfold,
Of journeys taken, brave and bold.
With every step, the past awakes,
In the darkness, the heart forsakes.

Stars ignite in the velvet sky,
Illuminating paths to fly.
As shadows merge with the dawn's embrace,
New beginnings find their place.

The night retreats, but we remain,
In shadows reclaimed, we feel no pain.
Our spirits rise, a rebirth song,
Together, we have found where we belong.

So hold my hand, let the journey start,
In every shadow, you find your heart.
A tapestry woven with dreams untold,
In the shadows reclaimed, we are bold.

The Weight of Gentle Hands

In the morning light, soft and warm,
Gentle hands weave dreams from the storm.
With every touch, a silent vow,
To hold each moment, here and now.

A tender heart knows all the aches,
Yet in its strength, the spirit wakes.
Through trials faced and burdens shared,
The weight of love is always bared.

When shadows loom and doubts arise,
Gentle hands become our skies.
In fragile whispers, comfort grows,
In the weight of care, the heart knows.

With every tear, a story flows,
Where the heart breaks, kindness grows.
A steady grip, a lullaby,
The weight of gentle hands, we fly.

Together we'll navigate the bends,
In the depth of love, we find our ends.
For in each ounce of gentle grace,
The weight of hearts finds its place.

Rebirth from Ashes

In fire's glow, the night heals pain,
From ashes cold, we rise again.
With every ember, dreams ignite,
A phoenix soaring, taking flight.

The heart remembers what was lost,
Yet clearer skies reduce the cost.
In the canvas of the dawn,
Rebirth whispers, we are reborn.

From silent fears to fierce embrace,
We carve the past, we find our place.
With every flame, new stories weave,
In the ashes, we learn to believe.

Together we stand, strong and free,
In every heartbeat, destiny.
The spirit rises, light anew,
From ashes born, we find our true.

So let the fire dance and soar,
For rebirth beckons, forevermore.
In cycles of love, hope will last,
From ashes, we are free at last.

Echoes of Breathe

In the stillness of the night,
Whispers dance with the stars,
Carried on winds of hope,
Breathing life into dreams.

Nature's lullaby sings soft,
Crickets play their gentle tune,
Each sound a fleeting moment,
Captured in the dark's embrace.

Fleeting shadows come and go,
Memories etched in silence,
Echoes of laughter linger,
Fading into the twilight.

With each heartbeat, we rise up,
Unraveling threads of the past,
Embracing the warmth inside,
As morning breaks the stillness.

A new dawn whispers softly,
Awakening the weary soul,
Together we find our strength,
As we breathe, we become whole.

Constellations in Our Skin

We wear the stars upon us,
Patterns born from ancient light,
Each mark a tale of longing,
Constellations spun in dreams.

Flecks of gold and silver lines,
Crisscrossing the canvas bare,
Stories of a thousand lives,
Written in the depths we hide.

In every scar, a memory,
In every freckle, a wish,
Together they form our map,
Guiding us through the dark.

Hand in hand, we chart the skies,
Navigating with our hearts,
The universe within us,
Twinkling in the night's breath.

Together we find our way,
Painting dreams across the void,
In the glow of our embrace,
Constellations in our skin.

The Alchemy of Emotions

In the crucible of the heart,
Feelings turn to liquid gold,
Each tear a precious moment,
Fleeting yet so deeply bold.

Joy sparkles like the sunrise,
Hope blooms in the coldest night,
Sorrow weaves a tapestry,
A reminder of our fight.

With every breath, we transform,
Alchemy of soul's design,
Turning hurt to understanding,
In shadows, our light will shine.

We gather fragments of our past,
Molding them with tender care,
In the process, we discover,
The beauty of being bare.

Together, we rise from ashes,
Forging bonds of strength anew,
A symphony of our feelings,
In the alchemy of me and you.

A Canvas of Recovery

Strokes of color paint the dawn,
Healing blooms on every page,
With each stroke, a story born,
A canvas shaped by every age.

We blend the hues of sorrow,
Add whispers of the light,
Brushing fears into the past,
As we craft our future bright.

In the silence, we find voice,
Dangling dreams on tattered threads,
Each layer holds a choice,
Guided by the paths we tread.

With every heartbeat, we invest,
The masterpiece unfolds with time,
In our hands, the power rests,
To create our cherished rhyme.

Together, we paint our stories,
A tapestry of the soul,
In the art of recovery,
We find the strength to be whole.

Fragments to Wholeness

In quiet corners, shadows play,
Scattered dreams drift far away.
Pieces lost in time and space,
Yet in chaos, find a trace.

Every shard tells a story bold,
Whispers of warmth in the cold.
With each step, the fragments blend,
A journey learned, a heart to mend.

A tapestry of sights unseen,
Threads of joy, spaces between.
Together, they create the art,
Finding solace in the heart.

In the puzzle, we are whole,
Connecting pieces, soul to soul.
Life's fragments can often shine,
Creating beauty, pure and fine.

So gather sparks from scattered light,
Bring them close, embrace the night.
For in every broken part,
Lies a path to a brand new start.

Stitches of Tomorrow

With needle sharp, we thread the day,
Sewing dreams in hues of gray.
Each stitch a hope, each knot a prayer,
For a future that waits right there.

Fingers dance on fabric fine,
In the creation, we intertwine.
Moments wrapped in warm embrace,
Around our fears, we find our place.

Time ticks by, and we create,
A canvas broad, a woven fate.
Through the struggles, hands withstand,
Stitches forming a steady hand.

Each thread a story, a silent vow,
We stitch together, here and now.
In the making, life unfolds,
A tapestry of dreams retold.

So let us wrap the world in light,
With threads of love, we'll take flight.
Hand in hand, we'll weave and sew,
Our tomorrow's bright, let it glow.

Candid Confessions of a Heart

The heart whispers secrets deep,
In shadows where emotions sleep.
Each beat a truth, raw and bare,
In the silence, we lay it there.

Candid tales of joy and pain,
Love's sweet sunshine, loss's rain.
Tender moments, scars that stay,
In the light, they fade away.

With gentle words, we uncover,
Stories shared, a bond, a lover.
Confessions spill like morning dew,
Each drop a glimpse of what is true.

In honest voices, barriers fall,
Bringing strength, we rise tall.
The heart, a mirror, reflects the soul,
In vulnerability, we find whole.

So let the truth be our guide,
In every heartbeat, love won't hide.
With open hearts, let's intertwine,
Candid confessions make us shine.

The Color of Resilience

When storms gather, skies turn gray,
Resilience blooms along the way.
In every challenge, colors emerge,
Painting life with a vibrant surge.

With every fall, we stand anew,
Brush strokes bold in shades of blue.
Through the struggle, light breaks through,
A vivid canvas of me and you.

In the depths, we find our grace,
Colors woven in a strong embrace.
Each hue a story, fierce and bright,
Reflecting strength in the darkest night.

The heart holds scars as badges worn,
Proof of battles fought and torn.
Yet every line, a tale to tell,
In the color, we rise, we fell.

So splash your canvas, let it glow,
With hues of courage, let it show.
For in resilience, beauty forms,
A masterpiece against the storms.

The Broken Pathway

A path once bright, now worn and gray,
With every step, the shadows sway.
Whispers of loss in the tangled wood,
Dreams once bright now misunderstood.

Twisted roots crown the weary ground,
Echoes of laughter no longer found.
Silent at dusk, the old trees sigh,
In the stillness, time slips by.

Footprints faded, leading astray,
Searching for light in disarray.
Hope flickers dim, yet still, it glows,
Amongst the thorny overgrows.

Nature grieves where joy once danced,
In shadows deep, lost souls entranced.
But in the dusk, a promise stirs,
Life finds a way, despite the slurs.

A journey carved through pain and strife,
Fragments of heart tell tales of life.
Even in darkness, stars will gleam,
Guiding the lost towards their dream.

In the Aftermath of Rain

Softly drips the silver dew,
Nature's tears now kissed anew.
Puddles form in glistening light,
Reflecting hope after the night.

Leaves tremble in the gentle breeze,
Singing songs beneath the trees.
Colors bloom in vibrant cheer,
Whispers of joy for all to hear.

Clouds retreat, the sky grows clear,
Nature's canvas now sincere.
Freshly washed, the world awakes,
Life reborn in tender stakes.

In every droplet, stories told,
Of warmth and life, both brave and bold.
A symphony of peace resounds,
In the aftermath of joy that surrounds.

So breathe the air, feel the embrace,
Each moment held in nature's grace.
After the storm, beauty shall reign,
In the afterglow, hope will remain.

Pages of Restoration

Turn the leaf, a new dawn breaks,
In chapters filled with love's mistakes.
Ink may bleed, but hearts can heal,
Finding strength in what is real.

With every story penned in time,
We mend the threads, so intertwined.
Sorrow shared becomes a song,
In unity, we all belong.

Blank pages hold the dreams undone,
Yet in silence, courage can run.
Through trials faced and battles fought,
Pages turn where lessons are taught.

We write the tales of joy and tears,
A saga shaped by hopes and fears.
In every word, a whisper of grace,
Restoration found in each embrace.

So let us ink the truth we find,
On pages filled with heart and mind.
For in the story, we lay bare,
The power of love, always there.

The Heart's Quiet Awakening

In shadows deep, a whisper stirs,
Quietly, the heart prefers.
Gentle beats in muted light,
Awakening from endless night.

Tender moments softly tread,
Memories of warmth long fled.
In silence deep, a sparkle glows,
As hope unfurls, love gently grows.

A fluttering breeze, the soul ignites,
In stillness found, the heart ignites.
From dormant days to vibrant hues,
Life springs forth with each new muse.

Embrace the dawn with open arms,
For in the quiet, tender charms.
The heart's awakening softly sings,
A melody of precious things.

So listen close to what you feel,
In tranquil moments, truths reveal.
The heart's quiet song shall say,
Love finds a way, come what may.

A Journey Beyond the Bruise

Through shadows deep, we walk anew,
A path of hope, with skies so blue,
Each bruise a tale, each scar a song,
In strength we rise, we shall belong.

With every step, the weight will fade,
In battles lost, we find our trade,
Resilience blooms where pain once lay,
A journey lit, come what may.

The echoes whisper of dreams untold,
In every heart, a fire bold,
We shed the past, embrace the dawn,
With courage firm, we journey on.

Through valleys low and mountains tall,
We stand together, we will not fall,
With every bruise, a brighter hue,
We find our strength, our truth anew.

And when we look back at all we've crossed,
We'll count the wins, forget the lost,
For in this life, with all its strife,
We've crafted something deep as life.

Blooming Despite the Storm

In darkest nights, a bloom will rise,
With petals bright against the skies,
The storms may howl, the thunder break,
Yet still, we grow for our own sake.

The winds may bend, but not destroy,
Our roots hold firm, a steadfast joy,
Through rain and hail, we find our place,
In nature's arms, a warm embrace.

Each raindrop sings a gentle tune,
A symphony beneath the moon,
We stand as one, in storms we thrive,
With every struggle, we feel alive.

The sun will shine, the clouds will part,
Resilient blooms from fragile heart,
Together we dance in wild delight,
Forever reaching for the light.

So let the winds come, fierce and wild,
We'll face the tempest, nature's child,
For in the storm, we truly see,
The strength in us, wild and free.

The Softest Embrace

In quiet moments, hearts entwine,
A gentle touch, so sweet, divine,
With each caress, the world stands still,
In love's embrace, we find our will.

Through whispered words and tender sighs,
We weave our dreams beneath starlit skies,
With every heartbeat, the silence breaks,
In every breath, love's rhythm wakes.

Despite the chaos, soft and true,
Your arms, a haven, ever new,
A shelter found in storms of night,
In the softest embrace, we're infinite light.

All fears dissolve, like mist at dawn,
In your embrace, I am reborn,
Through trials faced, we stand as one,
In tender warmth, the battle's won.

So let the world around us fade,
In every heartbeat, our love unmade,
For in this softness, we shall stay,
Forever bound, come what may.

From Ashes to New Growth

Amidst the ruins, life takes flight,
From ashes gray, new blooms ignite,
With every ember, hopes are sown,
In darkest times, our strength is shown.

The fire's fury left scars behind,
Yet from the smoke, new paths we find,
With roots that dig in charred remains,
We rise anew, despite the pains.

Each leaf unfurling tells a tale,
Of past endured, of love's prevail,
In courage found, we reach for sky,
Together, we embrace the high.

So let the storms come bend and break,
For in each trial, we learn to wake,
With every dawn, the earth will sing,
From ashes strong, new life will spring.

With every breath, we break the chains,
Unfurl the dreams from deepest pains,
For in the ashes, hope is bound,
From loss, new growth will wear the crown.

Beneath the Surface

Beneath the ripples, secrets lie,
Whispers of dreams, lost in the tide.
The depths hold stories, old as the sky,
Awaiting the brave, who drift and glide.

In shadows made soft by the moon's glow,
Words unspoken, linger like dust.
Only the heart knows where to go,
As echoes of past slowly adjust.

Coral beds hug the sea's embrace,
Life pulsates in elegant dance.
Every creature finds its place,
In this realm of fate and chance.

Ripples carry the weight of the past,
Glimmers of hope, the future's lore.
Tides will turn, but the memories last,
Beneath the waves forevermore.

Awake to the world beyond the foam,
Every sigh beneath the azure dome.
In tranquil depths, we find our home,
And rise anew, wherever we roam.

The Unfolding Journey

Each step we take, a path unknown,
Full of twists, like a winding road.
With every turn, seeds are sown,
In the soil of dreams, where wanderers strode.

Mountains loom vast, skies stretch wide,
With courage stitched in threads of gold.
The heart anchored in steadfast pride,
As stories of old in whispers unfold.

Through valleys deep and rivers clear,
Each moment a compass, guiding our way.
Together we trudge, facing the fear,
Embracing the light of each coming day.

Every face met, a chapter penned,
Fellow travelers carving the light.
In friendship we find, a means to mend,
As together we chase the stars at night.

The journey continues, no end in sight,
With dreams carried forth, as brave as the dawn.
With each new horizon that greets our flight,
We step boldly forth, and the past is reborn.

Silence of the Phoenix

In the hush of dawn, where ashes lie,
A whisper of wings, soft in the air.
From embers deep, the spirit will fly,
In a blaze of color, wild and rare.

With feathers aflame, it rises anew,
Transcending the depths of silent despair.
Each note resounds, a triumph so true,
As shadows retreat from the fiery flare.

Once lost in the dark, a tale of grief,
Now burns with the colors of day's gentle light.
From silence springs forth, sweet golden relief,
As the phoenix ascends, a heart taking flight.

Through whispers of past, the echoes remain,
Scarred beauty shines through every rebirth.
In silence, it dances, shedding the pain,
A testament forged in this vibrant earth.

Embrace of the flames, a radiant plight,
Illuminated truths, in the stillness declare.
The phoenix will rise, borne up by the night,
In the silence of power, we find what is rare.

Rise and Reimagine

In moments of stillness, dreams ignite,
Soft embers glow, waiting to spark.
With the dawn's kiss, we shed the night,
As visions whisper, guiding each heart.

Walls built high now crumble away,
Casting shadows of doubt to the ground.
In the open air, we find our sway,
With breath anew, we dance and rebound.

Each thought a thread, weaving the light,
Colors unfurl in the tapestry wide.
With courage to rise, we step into flight,
As hope's gentle hand becomes our guide.

Together we bloom on this journey we share,
Reimagining futures with passion and grace.
Through trials faced, we strip down to bare,
Finding strength in the love we embrace.

So rise, dear soul, let your spirit soar,
Rewrite your lines; let the world feel your fire.
In unity bound, we gather and roar,
Reimagine the path to our hearts' desire.

In the Wake of Suffering

Broken dreams lie scattered wide,
Echoes of the tears we cried.
Yet in darkness, seeds can grow,
Hope emerges, soft and slow.

Silent strength beneath the pain,
Wounds will heal, we rise again.
Each step forward, courage found,
In the wake, new grace unbound.

Through the storm, we learn to bend,
Every heartache leads to mend.
In the shadows, light breaks through,
Suffering births a stronger view.

Fallen leaves, a path now clear,
With each breath, we face the fear.
Together, hand in hand we stand,
Rebuilding lives across the land.

Resilient hearts, we choose to soar,
And find the joy we longed for more.
In the wake, with spirits bright,
We kindle flames from darkest night.

Footprints in the Dirt

Footprints marked along the way,
Stories told in soft decay.
Every step, a tale unfolds,
Memories carved in subtle molds.

The sun will shine, the rain will fall,
In nature's dance, we hear the call.
Footprints fade, yet spirits stay,
Guiding us through every day.

Winds will whisper through the trees,
Sending echoes on the breeze.
Paths once traveled, lost in time,
Yet in our hearts, they still rhyme.

With every journey, lessons learned,
In quiet corners, fires burned.
The dirt remembers where we've been,
Each footprint left, a silent grin.

From dusk till dawn, we journey on,
With dreams alive, never gone.
Footprints linger, soft and bright,
A testament of hope and light.

When Splinters Turn to Gold

In the workshop of the soul,
Splinters gather, take their toll.
Beauty forged through rugged pain,
Crafting strength from every strain.

Dust and sweat, the artist's gain,
Transforming hurt, embracing rain.
What was lost becomes a gem,
When splinters turn to golden stem.

Each scar tells a tale of fight,
Turning shadows into light.
With every flaw, a story spun,
In the chaos, hope begun.

Hands that tremble at the start,
Seeding courage in the heart.
When life's trials take their toll,
We find treasures deep and whole.

From broken pieces, we create,
A mosaic of love, not hate.
Splinters shine, a truth so bold,
In the turmoil, hearts unfold.

The Gentle Unraveling

Threads of life, in gentle flow,
Woven tightly, then they go.
In stillness, soft whispers call,
Embracing secrets, big and small.

With every twist, a tale released,
The journey bends, yet never ceased.
Patterns change, as we explore,
A dance of hearts, forevermore.

Layers shed like autumn leaves,
Revealing truths that nature weaves.
In the unraveling, we find grace,
Embracing time's unhurried pace.

Gently stripped of what we hold,
New beginnings start to unfold.
In the quiet, dreams will bloom,
A gentle light dispels the gloom.

Through the chaos, peace arrives,
In the soft, the spirit thrives.
The gentle thread that binds us tight,
Unraveling, we find our light.

Whispers of Renewal

In the still of dawn's embrace,
Nature breathes a tender sigh,
Petals unfold with gentle grace,
Underneath the vast, bright sky.

Hope springs forth from every seam,
Awakening the dormant dreams,
A melody of life's soft theme,
Flowing like the crystal streams.

Birds take flight on whispered wings,
Carving trails in morning light,
Nature hums while softly sings,
A promise born from endless night.

Each leaf a tale of what has been,
Yet shines bright in the sun's soft glare,
In every loss, a chance to win,
Renewal found in loving care.

So listen close to softest sounds,
For in the quiet, truth appears,
With every heartbeat, life rebounds,
Whispers of renewal through the years.

Bandages of Time

With every tick, the world does mend,
Moments stitched in memory's thread,
Time's gentle hand, a loyal friend,
Heals the wounds, the tears we've shed.

Rustling leaves and aged oak trees,
Whisper stories of days gone by,
Comfort lingers in the breeze,
As echoes of the past drift high.

Faded photographs held tight,
Captured smiles in fragile frames,
Each image tells of love and light,
Bandages for the heart's deep claims.

Through every wound, a lesson learned,
In trials faced, strength is found,
Hope ignites, brightly burned,
In every heartbeat, life unbound.

With every scar, a tale to tell,
Time weaves softly through the fray,
In the heart, where memories dwell,
Bandages of time guide the way.

Echoes of Resilience

In every struggle, strength is born,
A spark that lights the darkest night,
From ashes rise, the spirit, worn,
Yet standing tall, prepared to fight.

Waves may crash and winds may howl,
Yet deep within, a fire glows,
Through every trial, the heart will howl,
Resilience blooms, the spirit grows.

With unwavering faith, we tread,
Navigating storms with grace,
For every tear that we have shed,
Becomes a part of our embrace.

A symphony of voices rise,
In unity, we find our way,
Together, strong, we touch the skies,
Echoes of resilience at play.

With every step, a testament,
To endurance in the face of fear,
In every heart, a fierce intent,
To thrive, to love, to persevere.

The Art of Mending

With needle poised and thread in hand,
A tapestry of dreams begins,
Stitch by stitch, we take our stand,
In every loss, a chance to win.

The fabric torn, yet not undone,
Each patch a story, woven tight,
Underneath the morning sun,
A masterpiece finds its own light.

Hearts that break can still be whole,
Through loving whispers, kindness shown,
In every crack, a deeper soul,
The art of mending brightly grown.

With every tear, a lesson learned,
For beauty lies in every scar,
A journey where the heart has turned,
Towards healing found in who we are.

So take your time, embrace the art,
Of stitching life with hope and grace,
For every moment plays a part,
The art of mending we embrace.

Serenity in the Struggle

In the depths of the night, I find my peace,
Whispers of hope that never cease.
Beneath the weight, I learn to rise,
Finding strength in the silent skies.

Every storm that I face, I embrace,
Through the chaos, I carve my space.
With each challenge, a lesson earned,
In the fire, my spirit burned.

I dance in the shadows, light my way,
Each heartbeat a promise, come what may.
The beauty found in pain's embrace,
In struggle, I bloom, I find my place.

As dawn breaks gently, I breathe anew,
Colors of courage in morning's hue.
Though the road is long, I'm not afraid,
With serenity found, I am remade.

Reflections of a Journey

Footsteps etched in the sands of time,
Every path taken, every rhyme.
Memories linger, like stars in the night,
Guiding my heart, filling it with light.

Mountains climbed, valleys crossed wide,
With trials behind, I carry my pride.
Lessons learned in each twist and turn,
For each lost page, a new one in turn.

Waves of doubt crash against my shore,
But I stand tall, wanting more.
Reflecting on moments, both bitter and sweet,
Each chapter unfolds with a new heartbeat.

As I glance back at the road I've paved,
Grateful for all the love I've saved.
With every smile, a story to tell,
In the journey of life, I blossom and swell.

The Scent of Fresh Beginnings

Morning dew hangs on petals bright,
The world awakens in soft sunlight.
Whispers of spring float in the air,
Inviting dreams, free from despair.

Each sunrise paints a canvas anew,
Hopes unfurling, a vibrant hue.
With every breath, I feel the thrill,
Of possibilities waiting to fill.

The scent of blossoms, sweet and pure,
Reminds me of futures that feel secure.
Carefree laughter dances on the breeze,
In this moment, my spirit is at ease.

I plant my seeds in the fertile ground,
With faith in the journey, joy will abound.
As I nurture dreams into the light,
Fresh beginnings bloom, a beautiful sight.

Growing Through Grief

In the shadow of loss, I find my heart,
A journey of healing, a brand new start.
Memories linger, like whispers in time,
In each tear shed, a reason to climb.

Roots interwoven, strong yet frail,
Through sorrow's embrace, I learn to sail.
Each moment cherished, each laugh, a gift,
In the cracks of my heart, I begin to lift.

With every sunset, a promise made,
That love does not fade, it will not trade.
In the tapestry woven, threads intertwine,
Grief nurtures growth, a love divine.

I carry their spirit in all that I do,
With every heartbeat, I feel them anew.
From the ashes of pain, a flower will bloom,
In growing through grief, I find room.

Beyond the Bruises

In shadows deep where sorrows linger,
A heart can mend, though pain grows stronger.
Each mark a tale of battles faced,
Yet courage blooms with delicate grace.

Beneath the weight of heavy sorrow,
Hope whispers softly of a bright tomorrow.
With every tear, a lesson learned,
In the ashes, a fire burns.

The journey's long, but steps stay light,
Through darkest days, we seek the light.
Beyond the bruises, scars will fade,
Resilience forged, a brave upgrade.

In tender moments, love takes flight,
Together we'll dance, through endless night.
A tapestry of strength we weave,
In our hearts, we choose to believe.

So here's to us, in every fight,
Emerging strong, holding on tight.
With each dawn, a chance to rise,
Beyond the bruises, we touch the skies.

Seasons of Renewal

In quiet woods where whispers flow,
The seeds of change begin to grow.
Spring's gentle hand draws life anew,
Awakening dreams, the world imbues.

Summer's warmth paints colors bright,
Golden days and starry nights.
In laughter shared, our spirits soar,
Together we bloom, forevermore.

Autumn leaves in hues of fire,
Whisper tales of sweet desire.
Change beckons softly, yet bold,
In letting go, new stories unfold.

Winter rests with quiet grace,
In peaceful stillness, we find our place.
Within the frost, hope always hides,
For every end, a new path bides.

Through seasons passed, our roots run deep,
With every cycle, memories we keep.
In nature's rhythm, we learn to play,
Embracing life, come what may.

The Sweetest Resilience

When storms do rage and shadows gleam,
In the darkest hours, we still dream.
Like fragile blooms that bend yet stand,
Our spirits rise above the sand.

Each struggle brings a deeper grace,
In every challenge, we find our place.
With laughter bright as morning's glow,
We rebuild strength from every blow.

With open hearts, we share our scars,
And find our way beneath the stars.
The sweetest strength is forged in pain,
Through every loss, our hope remains.

In unity, we learn to thrive,
Connected souls, so alive.
We dance through life, with hearts entwined,
In love's embrace, true peace we find.

So when the world seems cold and gray,
Remember the light will find its way.
With sweetest resilience, we stand tall,
Together, we shall never fall.

Petals in the Storm

Amidst the chaos, flowers bloom,
Petals dancing, dispelling gloom.
In every gust, a lesson found,
Resilient hearts, though shaken, sound.

Each drop of rain a story shared,
Of strength and beauty, deeply cared.
In fleeting moments, joy can rise,
Like fragile blooms reaching for the skies.

When tempests rage and shadows loom,
We stand as one, refusing gloom.
Hand in hand, we brave the night,
Together our spirits ignite.

For life's a whirlwind, bold and bright,
Through trials faced, we find our light.
Petals in the storm, we do not break,
With every challenge, our hearts awake.

So let the winds of change blow through,
With every breath, we start anew.
In storms we find the strength to grow,
As petals dance, our spirits glow.

Beneath the Weight of Time

Shadows stretch in the fading light,
Whispers echo, lost in flight.
Each moment drifts on silent wings,
Beneath the weight, the heart still sings.

Fragments of dreams in the twilight glow,
Memories linger, ebb and flow.
Time's gentle hands, they weave and sway,
Crafting stories that fade away.

Ancient echoes call from afar,
Carving paths through the evening star.
In the stillness, a truth is found,
Life's melody, a sacred sound.

Beneath the stars, we search the skies,
For answers wrapped in soft goodbyes.
The past and present intertwine,
Within each heartbeat, sacred sign.

To carry the weight, to rise and soar,
Finding meaning, always seeking more.
Through the journeys, we learn to be,
Eternally bound, you and me.

Symphony of Solace

In the quiet, where shadows play,
Gentle notes of night and day.
Softly strummed on heartstrings tight,
A symphony of calm takes flight.

Moonlight dances on the sea,
Whispers weave through the canopy.
Every star a note so bright,
Guiding souls to the morning light.

Breath by breath, the tension eases,
Nature's song, a balm that pleases.
With every pause, the world feels right,
Wrapped in warmth, a sheer delight.

In the stillness, peace is found,
In gentle echoes, love is crowned.
Harmony in the softest sigh,
A melody that will not die.

In the embrace of night's soft arms,
We find a refuge, shielded charms.
Eternal peace in whispered dreams,
A symphony, or so it seems.

Heartbeats and Horizons

Beyond the hills where shadows wane,
Heartbeats echo, sweet refrain.
With every dawn, we greet the day,
Chasing dreams that gently sway.

Horizons stretch in colors bright,
Softened edges, a glimpse of light.
Together we run, hand in hand,
In the warmth of a golden land.

With every step, we feel alive,
In the moments, we learn to thrive.
The rhythm of life, a steady tune,
Guided by stars and the silver moon.

Every heartbeat tells a tale,
Of love and loss, of courage frail.
In the vastness, we find our way,
With hope to lead, come what may.

As horizons bend and time unfolds,
We gather dreams like precious gold.
In the dance of life, we rise and roam,
Finding solace in every home.

The First Breath After..

The first breath after the storm,
A whisper of calm, a soft warm form.
Raindrops linger, kiss the earth,
Sign of renewal, sign of rebirth.

Leaves glisten in the fresh sunlight,
Hope awakens, taking flight.
In stillness, the world begins to heal,
In every heartbeat, love we feel.

Every moment, a chance to start,
To mend the broken, heal the heart.
As flowers bloom with colors bold,
Life's precious stories quietly unfold.

In the echo of silence, peace thrives,
A gentle reminder, we are alive.
Through the struggles, through the pain,
We find the strength to rise again.

So breathe in deep and let it go,
Trust in the journey, trust in the flow.
The first breath after, a sacred call,
In this beautiful chaos, we stand tall.

Ribbons of the Past

Threads of memory softly weave,
Whispers of love that we believe.
In faded photos, smiles reside,
Time's gentle hand cannot divide.

Laughter echoes through the years,
Captured moments, joy and tears.
Lessons learned from tales untold,
In our hearts, their warmth we hold.

The quiet corners, stories rest,
In every shadow, we invest.
Glimmers of hope in words once spoken,
Souvenirs of bonds unbroken.

Wrapped in visions, dreams take flight,
Embracing darkness, seeking light.
Ribbons flutter, memories swell,
In our lives, they weave their spell.

Though time may fade these strands away,
In our hearts, they forever stay.
Ribbons of the past, a vibrant thread,
Binding us to love that's fed.

The Lantern's Glow

In the twilight, lanterns gleam,
Illuminating night's soft dream.
Guiding souls through whispers dim,
A gentle beacon, hope won't swim.

Flickering flames in the cool night air,
Casting shadows, dancing fair.
Stories hidden in flickers bright,
Carrying wishes on silver light.

Each lantern's glow, a secret shared,
Among the lost, love has dared.
A path unveiled, a guiding hand,
With whispered promises, they stand.

Through darkest hours, they never fade,
Illuminating paths we've laid.
In every heart, their warmth remains,
Silhouettes formed in soft refrains.

So raise a lantern, let it shine,
Through trials faced, your heart align.
In every glow, a life will start,
The lantern's glow within our heart.

In the Quiet of Regrowth

In the stillness, seeds take root,
Bursting forth, a tender shoot.
Whispers linger on the breeze,
Life awakens from its freeze.

With each dawn, new hopes arise,
Beneath the dome of painted skies.
Nature's rhythm, soft and slow,
In the quiet, strength will grow.

Foliage unfurling, emerald bright,
Embracing warmth, absorbing light.
In humble soil, a dream unfolds,
Fragile beginnings transform bold.

Raindrops nourish, sunbeams play,
A dance of life in grand array.
Roots that reach, branches outspread,
An anthem sung, a path ahead.

In the stillness, beauty starts,
Regrowth ignites the waiting hearts.
From quietude, a life will soar,
In the quiet of regrowth, we restore.

Mosaic of the Heart

Fragments gathered, colors blend,
Each a story, a means to mend.
In every piece, a tale confined,
A mosaic formed, intertwined.

Shattered dreams and hopes anew,
In every glance, a view askew.
Blended patterns, rich and bright,
A tapestry woven in the light.

Each shard reflects a moment lost,
Beauty found despite the cost.
A canvas painted with our scars,
Etched in memories, beneath the stars.

With every breath, a piece is whole,
Rebuilding life, a soulful goal.
The art of love, imperfect grace,
In the mosaic, find our place.

So cherish pieces, big and small,
In the grand design, they stand tall.
A heartbeat echoes, vibrant yet,
In the mosaic of the heart, we're set.

When Shadows Fade

In the quiet dusk, we breathe,
Dreams take flight, like autumn leaves.
Whispers echo, soft and low,
Hope ignites, in the gentle glow.

Stars awaken, bright and bold,
Tales of courage yet untold.
With each step, we carve our way,
Embracing light, as shadows sway.

Moments linger, time suspends,
Hearts connect, where friendship mends.
Fading doubts, a distant sound,
In the warmth of love, we're found.

As the night begins to wane,
Softly sings the moon's refrain.
With open hearts, we find our grace,
In the dawn, we face the chase.

When shadows fade, we rise anew,
Bound by faith, with skies so blue.
Together we forge a brand new fate,
In the light, let us celebrate.

Echoing Heartbeats

In the haze of twilight's sigh,
Two souls dance, as stars reply.
Heartbeat echoes, a gentle sound,
In this rhythm, love is found.

Voices whisper, secrets shared,
Every moment, we prepared.
Time stands still, in this embrace,
Lost in wonder, in sacred space.

Through the storms, we find our way,
Guided by the light of day.
In the silence, truth unfolds,
With each heartbeat, our story holds.

Memories linger, like sweet song,
With every note, we both belong.
In the tapestry of night so deep,
Echoing heartbeats, dreams to keep.

As the dawn begins to break,
Promises made, we won't forsake.
Together in this dance, we play,
Echoing heartbeats, come what may.

Rebirth of the Spirit

In the stillness, a whisper calls,
To rise anew, where sunlight falls.
Casting off the weight of old,
In the warmth, our hearts unfold.

Through the shadows, we emerge,
Renewed strength, a vibrant surge.
With the dawn, we find our flight,
In the glow, we seek the light.

Nature's rhythm, a gentle guide,
In every heartbeat, we abide.
Old wounds heal, as new paths form,
In connection, we feel the warmth.

Embracing change, we shed the past,
In this freedom, we are vast.
Every moment, a chance to grow,
In the journey, let love flow.

Rebirth of spirit, brave and bold,
With each story, a tale retold.
In the dance of life, we find our way,
With open arms, we greet the day.

The Tapestry of Healing

Threads of time, woven tight,
In every color, shadows light.
Pain and joy, a dance they make,
In this tapestry, hearts awake.

Stitches formed with love and care,
In the fabric, we all share.
With each layer, stories blend,
In unity, we find a friend.

Healing journeys, paths unknown,
Through the storms, we have grown.
With each tear, new fabric we spin,
In the tapestry, we're woven in.

Colors brighten, slowly fade,
In the heart, we're unafraid.
Finding strength in every strand,
Together, we rise and stand.

The tapestry, a sacred space,
Holding whispers of every face.
In the end, we all embrace,
The healing thread, a warm trace.

Nature's Gift of Time

Leaves whisper secrets soft and low,
A river's flow, a timeless show.
Mountains stand, their shadows cast,
In nature's realm, the die is cast.

Seasons change, a cycle spun,
Beneath the moon, the stars have fun.
Time unfolds like a gentle breeze,
Nature's gift puts the heart at ease.

Sunrise paints the sky anew,
With golden rays, a bright debut.
In every petal, a story's told,
In nature's arms, we find pure gold.

Whales sing songs beneath the sea,
Echoing through eternity.
A world alive, in every chime,
Embracing life, the gift of time.

Together we roam, hand in hand,
In this enchanted, timeless land.
Ours is the spirit, wild and free,
Nature's gift—a symphony.

The Warmth in the Void

In silence deep where shadows dwell,
A flicker whispers, casting a spell.
Stars gleam brightly, stories untold,
In the void, their warmth is gold.

Cold winds howling, the night so long,
Yet in the darkness, we find our song.
Hearts ignited, fierce and bright,
Bringing warmth to the thick of night.

A gentle candle's soft embrace,
Illuminates this hallowed place.
With every heartbeat, the dark retreats,
In void's embrace, our spirit meets.

The moonlight dances on dreams we share,
In the stillness, we lay bare.
Through cosmic depths, true love will sail,
In the void, our hearts prevail.

Connected souls, against the storm,
Together we rise, forever warm.
In the silence, we've found our way,
The warmth in the void shall forever stay.

Verses from the Shadows

In the muted dark, whispers arise,
Secrets linger, hidden from eyes.
Shadows dance in the silver light,
Each verse born from the depth of night.

Echoes resonate, forgotten sounds,
In the silence, our hearts rebound.
The moon a witness, soft and pale,
To stories woven in silence frail.

Each flickering flame unveils a dream,
Lost in moments, like a flowing stream.
Through tangled branches, the truth will creep,
Verses bloom from the shadows deep.

A world unseen, yet ever near,
In the quiet, we confront our fear.
With every verse penned, hope ignites,
Illuminating the longest nights.

Together we dwell, 'neath the veil of dark,
Finding solace in each whispered spark.
In shadows, our stories take their flight,
Crafting verses from the depth of night.

Shelter Amongst the Ruins

Amidst the stones, where silence lies,
Ancient echoes, whispered sighs.
Crumbled walls, tales to tell,
Shelter found where shadows dwell.

Nature reclaims what time has lost,
In soft green hues, redemption's cost.
Through shattered dreams, new life will bloom,
In every crevice, dispelling gloom.

Memories linger in the dust,
Of hearts once bold, in love and trust.
Each ruin a canvas, a story spun,
Of lives intertwined, now slowly done.

Together we tread this sacred ground,
In every shard, our hopes are found.
Amongst the ruins, we make our peace,
Finding solace, our own release.

Time whispers soft in the fading light,
Together we stand, ready to fight.
In every crack, the beauty flows,
Shelter amongst the ruins grows.

The Silent Work of Time

In quiet moments, shadows creep,
Worn pages tell secrets we keep.
Soft whispers of the days gone by,
Time's gentle hand, it can't deny.

Each tick of the clock, it weaves our tale,
In hushed breaths, we find our trail.
With every dawn, we learn to climb,
A tapestry spun by the silent work of time.

Through seasons changing, hearts will mend,
Old wounds heal, allowing us to blend.
In the echoes of what once was ours,
The past glimmers like distant stars.

So cherish each moment, fleeting and bright,
For every shadow gives birth to light.
In the slow unfurling, we find our way,
Embracing the dusk, we welcome the day.

In dreams of tomorrow, we cast our hope,
With patience and love, we learn to cope.
Though time moves slowly, let it be kind,
For in its embrace, the peace we will find.

Portraits of Recovery

Each face tells a story of battle fought,
Of shadows and light, of lessons taught.
A journey through valleys, steep and wide,
In every heart, a phoenix inside.

Fingers trembling as they reach for dawn,
In the quiet, a new strength is drawn.
With every scar, there's an art to claim,
A canvas of courage, never the same.

These portraits of struggle, painted with grace,
Reflect the beauty in the human race.
Through laughter and tears, resilience grows,
In every heartbeat, the spirit knows.

Holding each other through the night,
We rise together, ready to fight.
With whispers of hope, our spirits soar,
In the gallery of life, we are evermore.

So gather the colors, the vibrant hues,
In the tapestry of healing, we choose.
Each story matters, every voice is clear,
Together we thrive, together we cheer.

Echoes of Past Battles

In the silence of night, the whispers rise,
Tales of old warriors, brave and wise.
The clash of steel, the cry of pain,
In the echoes, their legacies remain.

Through fields once soaked in tears and blood,
A history flows like a restless flood.
Memories linger, etched in stone,
Lessons of courage, never alone.

For every wound, there's a tale to tell,
Of strength and struggle, of living well.
In the shadows, a light refrains,
The heart remembers what it gains.

From ashes to glory, the stories unfold,
Of battles won, of hearts made bold.
In the realm of the brave, we find our way,
With honor and hope, we seize the day.

So listen closely, to the whispers near,
Embrace the wisdom, hold it dear.
For in the echoes of what has passed,
The future shines bright, our spirits steadfast.

The Resilience Within

In the depths of despair, we find a spark,
A flicker of light in the cold and dark.
With courage ignited, we rise once more,
To conquer the storms that rattle the shore.

Each setback a lesson, each failure a guide,
In the heart of struggle, we learn to abide.
With every heartbeat, the strength will grow,
In the garden of life, resilience will show.

Through trials we wander, through shadows we tread,
In moments of silence, the fierce are bred.
A whisper of hope calls out to our soul,
With grit in our hearts, we reclaim our whole.

So stand with conviction, embrace the unknown,
For from every fracture, new strength will be grown.
In the tapestry woven, our stories align,
In the dance of resilience, our spirits entwine.

So let the waves crash, let the winds howl,
With every challenge, we will not cowl.
For inside us all is a fire that spins,
The unyielding force of the resilience within.

Whispers of the Scar

In shadows soft, a tale unfolds,
Of battles fought, a spirit bold.
The scar it whispers, secrets deep,
Of nights awake, and dreams we keep.

Through silent skies, the echoes play,
Of moments lost, yet here to stay.
Each line a story, etched in time,
A testament, both grim and sublime.

When gentle winds begin to blow,
The scars may fade, but still we grow.
With every breath, a chance to heal,
To find the strength in what we feel.

Beneath the surface, pain resides,
Yet light will shine where dark abides.
Embrace the whispers, let them lead,
To paths of hope, where hearts are freed.

A journey marked by love and scars,
Through hidden fears and distant stars.
In every wound, a lesson lies,
In every tear, a new sunrise.

Beneath the Bandage

Beneath the bandage, stories hide,
Of sorrows faced, yet love applied.
Each layer tells a different part,
Of healing wounds and mending heart.

The tender hands that seek to mend,
In quiet hours, so they tend.
With whispers soft, they break the seal,
To uncover all that scars conceal.

A fragile trust, like petals bloom,
Emerging from the shadowed gloom.
In gentle light, the fears rescind,
As wounds reveal what hearts defend.

With every pull, the pain may rise,
Yet through the tears, a hope defies.
For in the struggle, strength is found,
In every heartbeat, love unbound.

Underneath, a vibrant pulse,
A life reborn, no longer dulled.
With every bandage come release,
A tender touch, a lasting peace.

Tender Roots of Renewal

In earth so rich, the roots dig deep,
Where shadows dance and secrets creep.
Tender shoots reach for the sun,
In quiet strength, the new begun.

Through trials faced, and storms endured,\nThe heart finds
grace, its spirit cured.
With each embrace of gentle rain,
The soul is washed of lingering pain.

New growth appears where pain once lay,
With colors bright, to greet the day.
These tender roots now intertwine,
In life's embrace, we learn to shine.

Hope takes flight on fragile wings,\nA testament to all life
brings.
In every bud, the promise glows,
Of joyful paths, where love bestows.

And in the garden of the heart,
Renewal starts, and fears depart.
With tender roots, we rise anew,
To dance in light, and skies so blue.

Echoes of Forgotten Pain

In whispers low, the echoes dwell,
Of battles fought, no one can tell.
Through shadows cast, the past remains,
The heartbeat of forgotten pains.

Yet in the void, a flicker glows,
Reminding us that healing flows.
In silence held, the truths arise,
Revealing strength beneath the skies.

What once was lost, now finds its way,
In gentle hues of night and day.
For every wound, the heart will mend,
With time, our spirits learn to blend.

The echoes fade, yet still they ring,
A melody, a song we sing.
In pain's embrace, we find our place,
A tapestry of love and grace.

So listen close, to tales of old,
In every scar, a story told.
For echoes linger, ever near,
A testament to all we bear.

Four Seasons of a Soul

In spring, a bloom of hope,
Awakening all that lies,
Gentle rains and sunlit days,
A dance beneath vast skies.

Summer brings a vibrant glow,
Joyous laughter fills the air,
Hearts entwined, no room for woe,
Life's warmth beyond compare.

Autumn whispers tales of change,
Leaves of gold fall to the ground,
A bittersweet, yet lovely range,
As moments echo all around.

Winter wraps in snowy hush,
Stillness settles, peace can reign,
In quiet, souls reveal their crush,
And dreams emerge from latent pain.

Four seasons flow in heart's embrace,
A journey of both joy and strife,
Each cycle leaves a lasting trace,
The seasons of our complex life.

Dreams that Speak

In slumber's grasp, where shadows play,
Whispers dance on moonlit streams,
Visions weave a vibrant fray,
A tapestry of our dreams.

Fragments of a world unknown,
Colors brush the midnight air,
Echoes of the heart's own tone,
A canvas painted with despair.

Silent screams and laughter's glee,
Merge in layers of the night,
In such chaos, we find key,
To secrets hiding in plain sight.

Each dream a door, each vision bright,
Guiding us through realms untold,
In their light, we take our flight,
Finding joy, finding bold.

Awake or sleep, the dreams still speak,
They guide us on this winding road,
In every tear, in every peak,
In whispered stories, love is sowed.

Harmony Amidst the Fracture

In chaos, beauty finds its form,
A melody within the pain,
Each broken piece, a rising storm,
Yet, harmony sings sweet refrain.

Notes may clash, yet hearts unite,
A symphony of hope and fear,
In dissonance, we find the light,
Together strong when feelings steer.

From darkness, stars emerge and shine,
A testament to love's embrace,
In every fracture, souls align,
Creating art from life's raw grace.

Through trials faced and battles fought,
Resilience blooms like flowers wild,
In every hardship bravely sought,
We find the strength of spirit, mild.

So let us sing through every clash,
In turbulence, our hearts will soar,
For in the midst of every thrash,
Harmony can open doors.

The Lightness of Being

In moments where the world stands still,
A breathless hush, the heart takes flight,
In gentle waves, we feel the thrill,
The lightness of being, pure delight.

Each fleeting whisper, every glance,
Awakens joy, a soft embrace,
In laughter shared, we find our chance,
To feel the world's enchanted grace.

No burdens tethered to our souls,
In presence, time begins to wane,
We dance with life, as music rolls,
In every heartbeat, freedom tame.

As shadows fade, our spirits rise,
We float through dreams, on wings of gold,
In love's reflection, we are wise,
Embracing stories yet untold.

The lightness of being is our song,
A melody that sways in air,
With every note, we all belong,
In unity, we truly care.

Cypress Roots and Worn Stones

Beneath the cypress, roots entwine,
Their ancient wisdom, old as time.
Worn stones whisper tales of the past,
Echoes of moments, too fragile to last.

The river flows, a gentle guide,
Carving paths where secrets hide.
In sunlight's glow, shadows dance,
Nature's grace, a fleeting chance.

Through tangled branches, dreams take flight,
In twilight's warmth, they find their light.
With every breath, the world unfolds,
Stories wrapped in silence, told.

The cypress stands, a sentinel true,
Guarding whispers of me and you.
In worn stones, our journeys blend,
Through nature's heart, we often mend.

Underneath the sky so wide,
Life's precious moments, we cannot hide.
With cypress roots and stones we tread,
In every path, our spirits spread.

A Journey Within the Twists

Winding paths lead deep within,
Curves and turns where dreams begin.
A journey taken, step by step,
Questions linger, secrets kept.

Through forests dense, a light glows bright,
Illuminating thoughts at night.
In shadows of the mind we roam,
Searching for that hidden home.

Each twist reveals another layer,
A heart's echo, a quiet prayer.
With every turn, the dangers grow,
But strength within begins to show.

Mountains rise to greet the sky,
In valleys deep, I learn to fly.
The journey twists, but I stand tall,
Embracing every rise and fall.

So onward through each winding way,
I find myself anew each day.
With every twist, a chance to see,
The beauty in this journey free.

The Art of Finding Peace

In quiet moments, still and clear,
I seek the calm that draws me near.
A breath, a sigh, the world slows down,
In this simplicity, I find my crown.

The art of peace is soft and sweet,
A melody where heartbeats meet.
In gentle waves, the worries cease,
Like petals falling, they find release.

In twilight's glow, a whisper soothes,
Embracing all that fits and grooves.
Through nature's grace, tranquility shines,
In every leaf, a spark that aligns.

Find comfort in the rustling trees,
In every breath, a fleeting breeze.
With open heart, the world expands,
Drawing peace from gentle hands.

So let the moments linger long,
In the stillness, we grow strong.
For peace is found, not sought in vain,
In every joy, in every pain.

Journey Through the Veil

A veil hangs soft, a curtain drawn,
Between the dusk and the dawning fawn.
Behind the fabric, stories lie,
Calling out as whispers sigh.

I step into this sacred space,
Each heartbeat quickens with grace.
Through winding paths, my spirit sways,
In shadows deep, the spirit plays.

Illuminated by stars so bright,
The veil becomes a canvas of light.
Each moment spent, a treasure rare,
Unveiling truths that linger there.

The journey calls, a siren's song,
To places lost, where I belong.
Through veils of dreams, my soul takes flight,
In endless nights, I find the light.

A tapestry woven with love and pain,
Each thread a lesson, joy, or strain.
Through every fold, I come to see,
The journey through the veil sets me free.

Underneath the Surface

Beneath the waves, a hidden grace,
Soft whispers stir in a quiet space.
Secrets dance in twilight's glow,
Within the depths, where few dare go.

Ghostly shadows paint the floor,
Echoes linger, tales of yore.
A world alive, yet dimly seen,
Life thrives where the light is lean.

Ripples form and fade away,
Like dreams that come to softly play.
In silence deep, the heart can feel,
The truth that's veiled, the hidden real.

Unraveling knots with gentle care,
The surface masks what lies elsewhere.
In hushed tones, the currents speak,
Their restless hearts, both brave and meek.

So heed the call of worlds unseen,
Embrace the dark, the in-between.
For underneath, we must explore,
The stories deep, forevermore.

Seasons of the Soul

Winter whispers with frosty breath,
A stillness wrapped in whispers of death.
Spring awakens with colors bright,
Buds unfurling in morning light.

Summer dances in golden rays,
Laughter echoes through sunlit days.
Autumn paints with crimson fire,
Leaves of change, we all desire.

In every turn, a lesson learned,
With every phase, the heart is turned.
Seasons flow like river streams,
Carving paths through tender dreams.

The cycle spins, a sacred rite,
We walk through shadows, seek the light.
Each moment births a chance to grow,
In seasons' grip, the spirit glows.

Listen close to nature's song,
In every change, we all belong.
Let the rhythm of time unfold,
As seasons weave their threads of gold.

Reflections in Still Waters

Calm and clear, the waters lie,
Mirroring the vast, blue sky.
In silence deep, the world retreats,
Where heart and nature softly meets.

Ripples fracture the tranquil frame,
Thoughts arise, no two the same.
An inner voyage, a gentle sway,
As visions drift and dance away.

The glassy surface hides the depths,
Each secret locked, each whispered breath.
Yet in the glance, there's truth to find,
Reflections of the heart and mind.

Stillness speaks in hues of grace,
Where worries fade without a trace.
Engulfed in peace, we learn to see,
The beauty of what's meant to be.

So peer beneath the waiting tides,
Where hope and wisdom gently bide.
In tranquil waters, we become,
The echoes of what we have sung.

The Dance of Restoration

Under the stars, we gather round,
In unity, our hearts unbound.
A dance of life, of loss and gain,
We weave our story through joy and pain.

Through trials faced and bridges burned,
The fire within us softly churned.
We find the strength to stand once more,
As seasons shift and spirits soar.

In every step, a healing thread,
Binding the scars where hope has bled.
With every twirl, we shed the weight,
Release the past, embrace our fate.

Harmony thrives in leaps and bounds,
Across the floor, our laughter sounds.
In rhythm found, our souls align,
The dance of life, both yours and mine.

Together we rise, with open hearts,
In this vast world where healing starts.
So take my hand, let spirits sway,
In the dance of restoration, we find our way.

9 789916 790731